LOVE ALL?

MICHAEL HEATH

D1369009

Also by
Michael Heath

A Load of Cock *(with Derek Alder)*
Automata
Published by A.P.Rushton
Great Bores
Starbores
Cartoon Library No.1
Cartoon Library No.6
Published by Private Eye
Michael Heath's Cartoons from Punch
Published by George Harrap

LOVE ALL?

Michael Heath's
cartoons from The Guardian

**Blond
&
Briggs**

First published in Great Britain 1982 by BLOND & BRIGGS in association with A. P. Rushton
Blond & Briggs Limited, Dataday House, Alexandra Road, London SW19 7JZ

Copyright © Michael Heath 1982

ISBN 0-85634-133-9

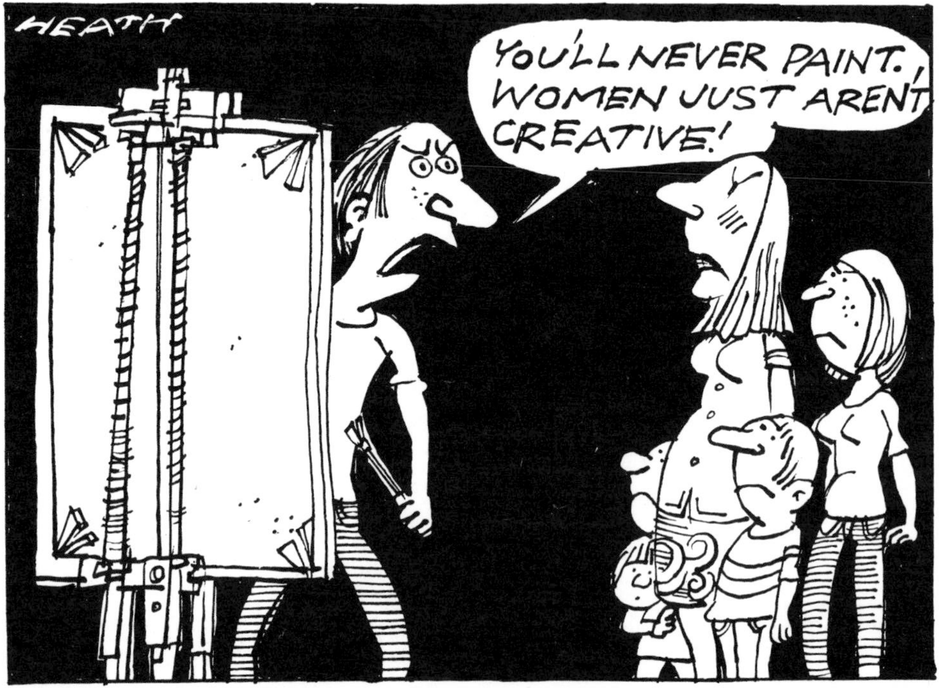
HEATH
YOU'LL NEVER PAINT. WOMEN JUST AREN'T CREATIVE!

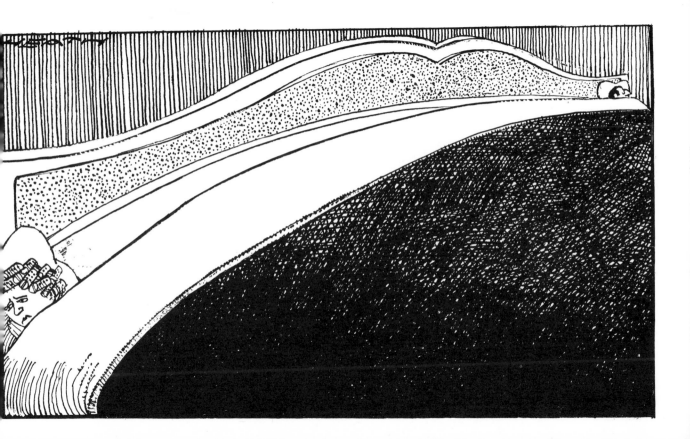

One Of Life's Little Puzzles

HEATH
MY HUSBAND AND I GET ON SO MUCH BETTER NOW THAT WE NEVER SEE EACH OTHER

Leaving Home

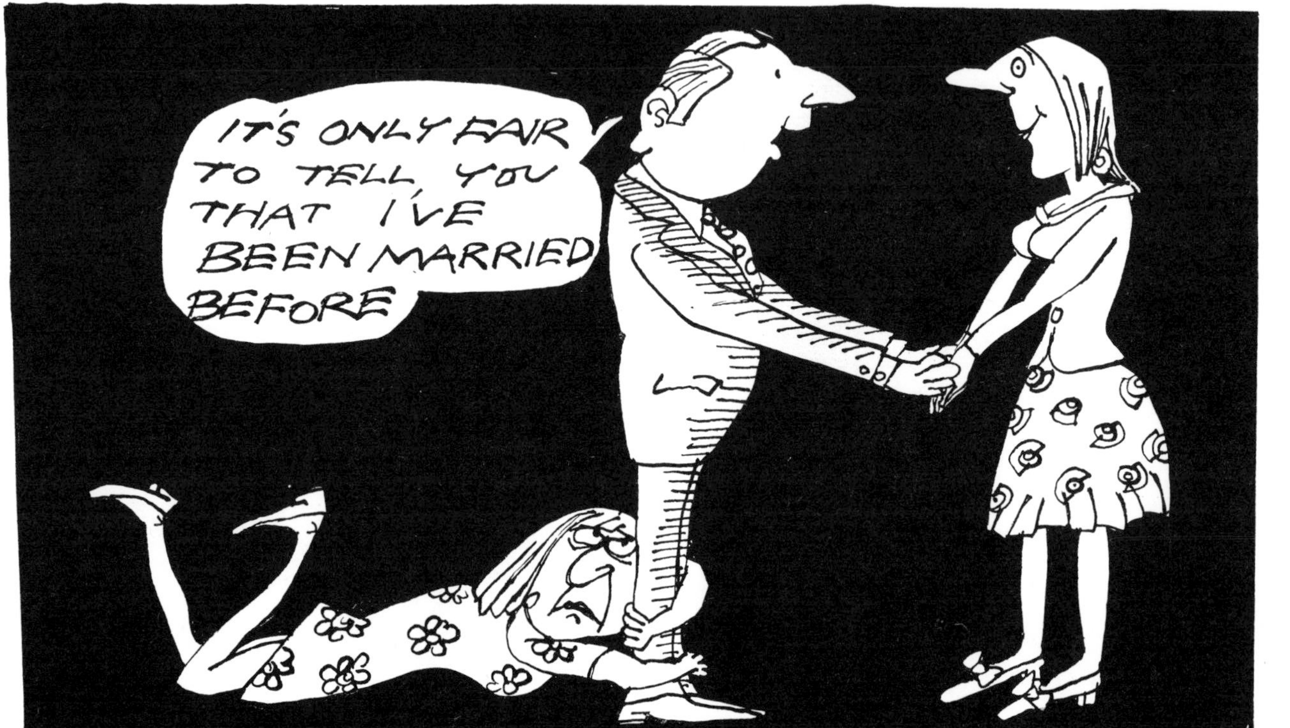
IT'S ONLY FAIR TO TELL YOU THAT I'VE BEEN MARRIED BEFORE

Joint Custody

OLD FOLKS HOME
THERE YOU ARE, I TOLD YOU YOUR HUSBAND WAS SLEEPING WITH ANOTHER WOMAN!
ZZZZZZZZZZZZZ
HEATH

NO, I DON'T WANT A GOOD TIME, BUT IF YOU COULD SEE YOUR WAY TO SEWING ON A FEW BUTTONS AND IRONING A SHIRT OR TWO....
STRIP
MADNESS
NF
HEATH

* MY WIFE DOESN'T UNDERSTAND ME!

Behind Every Successful Man There's A Good Woman

Familiarity Breeds Contempt

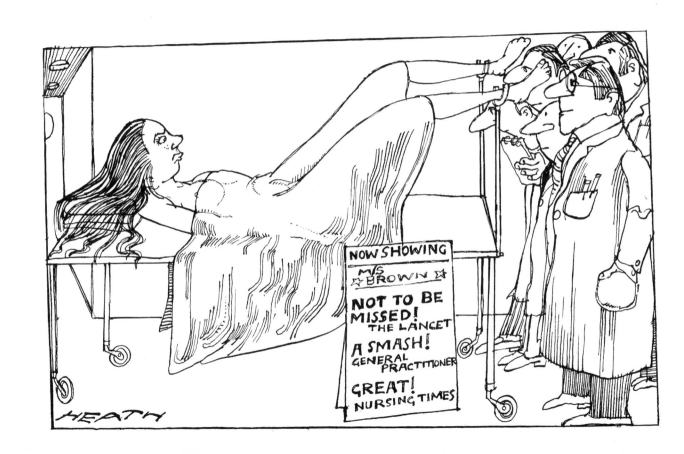

I'LL BE GLAD WHEN YOU GET OUT OF THIS PHASE, YOU'RE DRIVING ME CRAZY!
DAD
HEATH

Feeding Time

Girl Talk

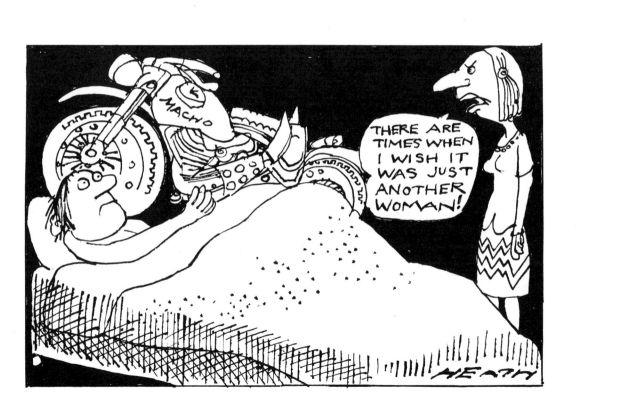

HEATH
ARE YOU SURE MARRIAGE IS SUPPOSED TO BE LIKE THIS DEAR?
WATER
BREAD

Love 40

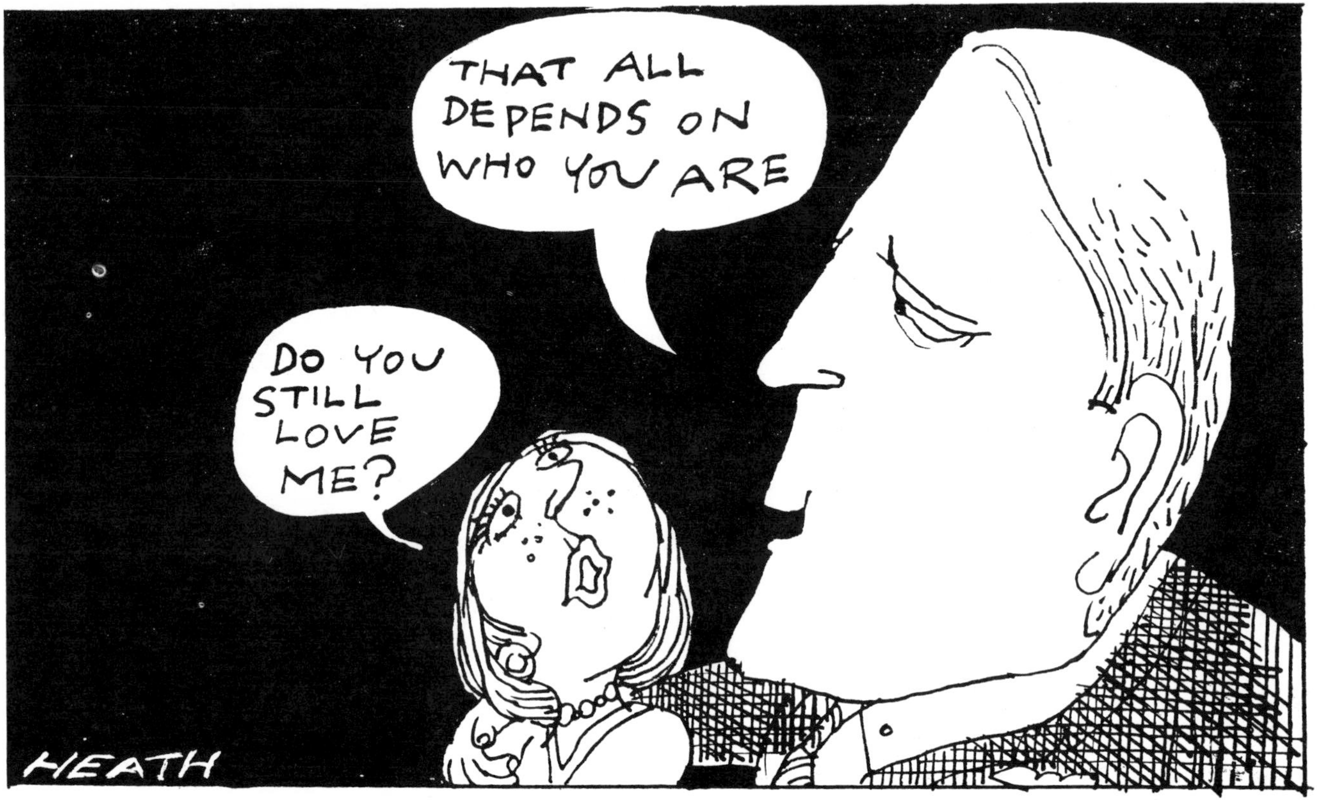
DO YOU STILL LOVE ME?
THAT ALL DEPENDS ON WHO YOU ARE
HEATH